the empress of the death house

THE EMPRESS OF THE DEATH HOUSE

by TOI DERRICOTTE

cover design...
JEANNE E. DERRICOTTE

calligraphy...
BARBARA VAN DYKE WOOD

LOTUS PRESS
Detroit

First Edition
First Printing

LOTUS PRESS
Post Office Box 601
College Park Station
Detroit, Michigan 48221

"Flower of a New Nile"

Acknowledgments

I wish to thank the editors of the following magazines and anthologies in which certain poems in this volume have previously appeared:

New Poets: Women: "the doll poem" and "the face/ as it must be/ of love"

Journal of New Jersey Poets: "sleeping with mr. death" and "the story of a very broken lady"

Gravida: "last will of one who lived alone" and "the naming"

Advance Token to Boardwalk: "the mirror poems"

New York Quarterly: "trees"

Pearl: "poem no. 1"

Buffalo Gnats: "The Grandmother Poems"

"unburying the bird" was awarded first prize in the Academy of American Poets competition at New York University.

                                                    T.D.

For my grandmother,
Marie Violet Webster,
as she lives in me.

Contents

I. SLEEPING WITH MR. DEATH

*"the hole of my mouth
grows darker"*

sleeping with mr. death

when you have hung the keys on the wall
& all you are left with is
mr. death
you untie his shoelaces
& roll him in
he is the shoulder you rub
on a cold night
he is the breath
you attend to
put your hand on his belly
& feel the stone bowels
he moves in the morning
measure the width
of his African nose
calculate the number of deaths
in his penis

you go down on him
he bursts in yr mouth
a thousand stars
flicker, then die

chalk-dry, mr. death

in the breeze from an open window
his bones
clatter like music

the story of a very broken lady

I.   the babies i have not been able to have
the slippery rubbery dolls
that have not been able to squeak through my thighs

i am splintery   i guard me like glass

i am old as dry kindling
i go up like an attic
belching my black smoke & fire

i must have praise
i must have praise like Our Lady

a light
must fall
on the ton
in my belly

No little ones to crack through my pelvis.
No little ones to crack me in two.

in my mother i choked on the chord
the out-going breath
struggled & caught

my voice snapped like a neck

so i make no music
i am jealous of my time
i tire like an old lady

they take me to the top of the stairs
remove my white shift
& stroke between my legs
to get the clear urine.

i am thistly   i itch like a monk's suit

II.   my house has become a secret
my children no longer speak to me
when i come home
they pass through me like ghosts

they are silent of comfort
they address me with the same respect
as dead ancestors

they turn away from me
like death in the future

i keep company under the hills
with scarves & with feathers
my O mouth for howling

nothing but crumbs & but slumber

my house is unfurnished
it is common as Howard Johnson's

it is the outside i turn to
windows
framing the view
like a woman's mahogany hair

15

nobody hears me
i talk & i talk

the walls close over me
my mother buries me
in the sound of her cooing

my father my doctor comes
bowing at my frightful pinkness
i am hot as pain
he keeps his hands off

he clucks like pigeons
he parades like fat roosters
he eats me like eggs

the bones of my tongue crack
on the roof of his mouth.

old troll lady,

old blankets & feathers
wave from my hole in the hill
wave my wild scarves
while the hole of my mouth
grows darker
& my speech is a sound
of no color

the mirror poems

Je vous livre le secret des secrets.
Les miroirs sont les portes par
lesquelles la Mort va et vient.

Cocteau

Prologue:

If she could only break the glass—
the silver is already peeled back like first skin
leaving a thin
transparent thing that floats across the ground
in front of her : this white shadow.

1. what a mirror thinks
    _____

a mirror thinks it has no self
so it wants to be everything it sees

it also thinks everything is flat

put a bunch together
& they think they see
the back side of the moon

17

2.   the mirror as a judge of character

keening my appetite
on the taste of an image of myself
sharpening myself
on bones;
suddenly
i lean over its eye
& see the way i see myself

i ask it
am i fairest in all the land

it opens like a backwards lake
& throws out of its center
a woman
combing her hair
with the fingers of the dead

3.   the mirror & suicide

someday
stand before a mirror & feel
you are drowned

let
your hair spread as sweet Ophelia's did
& you will rock
back & forth
gently
like a boat in kind water

18

4. questions to ask a mirror

remember:
whatever you ask a mirror
it will ask back

if you ask it
what will you give me
it will ask you
what will you give me

if you ask it what is love
it will turn into a telescope
& point at you

if you ask it what is hate
it will do the same thing

if you ask it what is truth
it will break in nine pieces

if you ask it what is beauty
it will cast no reflection

if you ask it to show you the world
it will show you the eye of your mother

5. conversing with the mirror

never tell a mirror you are black
it will see you as a rainbow
never tell a mirror you are white
it will make you disappear
in fact a mirror doesn't care
what color you are

19

never tell a mirror
how old you are
under 20
you draw a blank
over 40　it stares

never cry in front of a mirror
it gets cruel

if a mirror doesn't trust you
it squints

if a mirror hates you
it speaks in a high-pitched voice

if a mirror calls you long distance
don't accept charges　hang up

never run from a mirror
it always leaves a friend outside

never have sex with a mirror
you will have in-grown children

don't take money from a mirror
there are strings

if you must converse with a mirror
say to it:　you're pretty
& won't get broken

that gives you
7 years

6. the mirror & time
   _____

   the mirror IS NOT immortal
   in fact it only has nine lives:

   the first one is a thief
   the second a baker
   the third plays the harpsichord
   the fourth lives in the iron-bound
   section of newark &
   eats pork sausage
   the fifth predictably drinks
   the sixth goes into the convent
   but the seventh (this gets better)
   marries her father
   & humps up like a camel
   the eighth cries a lot and ZAP
   changes into a writer

7. the mirror & metamorphosis
   _____

   the eye   in the mirror   is the mirror   of the eye

8. the mirror & the new math
   _____

   inside the mirror
   opens up like the number zero
   you swim around in there
   bob up
   & drown
   like the rat in Wonderland's flood.   21

your tail would like to hook a reason,

but you keep coming
face to face
breast to breast
with yourself.

you fall backwards & away, even
think that you are lost
in Oceanic O,

but you are still
pinned to an inverse.

9. the mirror as a silent partner
───────────────────────────────

the mirror never talks
it is always astounded
with its O mouth open
& everything falling in

Epilogue:

Always straining toward her image, the girl
let go.

Tentacles of light
unlocked
like hooks of parasite

& she came back
in dark so dark,

she cannot see by sight

the face/as it must be/of love

i touch your nose
  & what beneath

the flesh mat
thick & soft
the brain grey as goat's curd
the kind cup of your skull

when will i break this mirror of your eye

in it

the moon
drags the water
on the shadow of its back

the earth
dims
like a jewel in darkness

& my face
hangs, starless
as dime-store crystal

divorcee

Men:
Beware the woman who thinks money will solve all her problems.

She thinks heaven is a man who works.

she has been bit so often in the cunt
she has sewn it closed

she spends her husband's money on cake
& drops trails to her best friend's house
she accuses him if he follows them
& accuses him if he doesn't follow them

she gets knocked up by her gynocologist
in order to have a free baby

she brings her daughters flatware, earrings, buttons
& anything that shines
she is teaching them to cover up the holes of death

she is teaching them to hate their father
because his sperm made them answerable to death

she is teaching them to marry a jewish doctor
or any man who has the proper fear of pregnant women

she is teaching them to buy geneology on time:
one cunt hair a month

she is teaching them to plant fly traps in their husband's shoes
& make sure he has double indemnity

she is teaching them to walk tall & carry his stick

she is teaching them to beat him with his stick

she is teaching them that eating eating eating
causes a woman to grow a penis

she is teaching great respect for fat ladies

she is teaching them to eat large amounts of fat
& secrete ambergris in their pants

   (her pants are slick
    & treacherous to climb)

she blasphemes teaches her daughters
that the first man splintered off eve's pelvis
& was born in a bag of pus

she is teaching them to reign in heaven and in hell

she is teaching them to measure their husband's penis
by something bigger than their husband's penis

she is teaching them to paint X's on the doors of churches
in menstrual blood

she is teaching them their skulls
screw open at night like telescopes
& let stars in

last will of one who lived alone

i have my freedom.
tip-toe around it
like an old maid's room.

my black silk fan
explodes with bird. 2
bisque ladies on a stand
curve
faultless as an unborn child.

i live here.

nothing needs me.

the air fern survives—
whether i live or die,
the dog makes it.

nights i curl up this bloodless sac—
a tic in the skin of the universe,
i will not move.

my appetite is what i know.

nun

I. Vacuumous,
the sun sets in yr mouth
yr tongue scales like an epileptic's
you swallow
before we can get the spoon in

yr belly, the inside
hot
as a live coal

the sun will never come up

it boils in the stew of yr stomach

the giblet of yr heart
soaks white
its red
mixes with the water
that pours from the wound of yr side

the edges
foam up like peroxide
you are ripped,
unzipped

in yr stomach
jesus stabs
the zig-zag stigmata.

II. She prays
     & bleeds
     all over the church

     a man in a black dress
     a closet faggot

     fucks her in the apse.

     cuckold of god,
     what is your claim to fame?

     that you can live totally
     on wafers of eucharist?

     that god drops
     manna in yr purse
     you can transform
     into subway tokens?

     that beneath the folds of yr scrupulosity
     yr hand
     can massage yr clit
     like a rosary?

     these beads
     these beads
     sister charity,

     are breaking up
     like globs of fat
     like fairway ducks
     with b.b.'s

Give up
sister charity
Go back

to the oak-soaked smell of the sixth grade—

    cleanliness
    & disrepute—

where mother superior
can check yr sins
in the womb of used laundry

& St. Cecilia, a 2nd century pin-up,
hangs on the wall of god's brothel
her hands on the piano
& jesus
plucking her strings

doll poem

doll is sitting in a box
she watches me
with 2 grey eyes
i take the top off
& look at her
she is wearing rubbers
to keep her feet dry
she is wearing eyeglasses
2 inches thick
she has padding on her soft behind
she is wearing excuses
all over
she is carrying threads
& buttons
she is a good hausfrau
prepared for all necessities
with kleenex
& kotex
& pencils
& lifesavers
& a boy doll with a wedding ring
she has lists as endless as dirt
     a grocery list
     a Xmas list
     a wine list
     a list of sins
     a list of movies
     a list of friends
her lists grow up
& eat lbs. of other lists

she is clean   clean   clean
she is rabbit quick
she copulates with ideas
she is good as gold
she is desirable as a tooth-fairy
she is the color of permanent
teeth
ask her her name
and turn her over
she says, ma ma

new lady godiva

she stops at the gas station
goes into the john &
unzips

her epidermis

peels out of it
skillfully
as a prostitute

long strips
slip to the pee-wet floor
& melt

like cotton candy

thus baptized
& pink as veal,

she goes to meet the public.

II. THE EMPRESS OF THE DEATH HOUSE

*"A masterpiece is a battle
won over death."*

Cocteau

poem no. 1

to hell with ezra pound
to hell with all you white-clad
men of the two-pronged dream
one   making love to rebecca   the other
gone down to sheba's to get sucked
damn you odysseus

i don't want to be yr cunt or consort
i don't want to genuflect to yr
        fop
worship at yr altars
where the toad-pricked assbishops
line up like unbaked pies

i'm thrice removed from the sacrosanct:

            the brat
          down the street
        nibbles like a rat
        at my kid's balls

                        today
he comes home from school
        and tells me—mama,
the kids at school say
        how can you be black
            when you got straight hair
              & white skin
you must be indian

remember when yr grandmother becky turned 14
   and the old master's son pushed her down in the field
   and took his first piece of ass
   becky didn't say a word
   and when her belly swoll up big as hell
  and the little bastard came out red your grandaddy
kissed it instead of smashing its head

the man wants more than love
he wants
  every oz.
    of juice
      yr body
        is capable
          of secreting

more than for you to kiss his turds
he wants you to save them for posterity

piss on you man:
last in a long
line of ass-
eaters
piss on this feast—

i want to come down on you
with my teeth   bite it
till the tendrils stand out
electrified
gorge on you like a teat
bathe in the black lake of yr blood
feast in yr groin

38

Trees

Hag Hand
Scratch sky

Devil foot
Grub earth

Outlive your babies:
Eat dog shit
And buried birds

The Grandmother Poems

The Empress of the Death House

My mother, bastarded by southern
greed; the rammed, inseparable
seed dyeing her cells,
married north.
I recall the weekly
visits to my grandmother's,
Webster's Funeral Home,
where we courted a northern
mother who hadn't yet put thumbs
up on any name but "Mrs. Webster."

Wednesdays, pinafored, packed
in blue velvet leggings from Saks
Fifth, we pegged the snow-long
blocks of Detroit's striving
colored Conant Gardens
to a last-ditch bus line
where we waited hours,
hopping back and forth on ice-
licked feet in a night of white
more blind than any other.

And sometimes, joking
about the red-striped mechanical
beast who slept remorseless
in his heated stall, we
turned and tunnelled
home.
Though I was only five,
and mother never said a word,
I wondered why

my grandmother,
green-eyed, henna-haired,
Empress of the Death House,
never launched her ship,
the Fleetwood, laying course
for far off Conant Gardens
where these cold survivors,
her inheritors,
waited clench-jawed, brass-clean
to perform their weekly rabbit scene.

The Feeding

My grandmother
haunted the halls
above Webster's Funeral
Home like a red-
gowned ghost. Til dawn
I'd see her spectral
form—henna-hair
blown back,
green eyes:
tameless.

She was proud.
Like God,
I swore I'd love her.
At night we whispered
how we hated mother
and wished that I could
live with *her*.

In the morning while she slept,
I'd pluck
costume diamonds
from a heart-shaped chest,
try her tortoise combs
and hairpins in my hair.
She'd wake
and take me to her bed.

Maroon-quilted, eider-downed,
I drowned.
Rocking on her wasted breast,
I'd hear her tell me
how she nursed my father
til he was old enough to ask.

Then, she'd draw me
to her—ask me
if she still had milk.
Yes. I said, yes.
Feeding on the sapless
lie,
even now
the taste of emptiness
weights my mouth.

The Funeral Parade

Over the Ambassador Bridge—
an arc of perpetual pregnancy—

we ride
to bury the dead.

Leading the way is one
blind, deaf, dumb:

the path has been cut,
we are doing our duty.

Grandfather,
in spats.

Grandmother,
tailor-made.

& the small child, the mourner,
blind as the buried.

the naming

(for Madeline Bass)

after 5 kids
she closed the shop

caught
a glimpse of herself
in a ginshe drama, a passion play

she wonders
if she is a martyr
or a fool

        (no, say what you mean)

i mean
i envy her

5
popping out of the juice hole
heads like jelly beans
monochromatic, pink,
5 with the vulnerability of sucked-out
easter eggs

i mean
she produced the scion
for her father to tie
the tail of his ape-man past
to his ape-man future

i mean   after 5
you simply
get tired

lie down in the dust
& count ants:

there's blood
in the semi-circular canal
swimming up to meet
the red pain in yr head

there are beasts
making all kinds of sounds at you,

& one
they keep repeating
over & over

until you finally recognize
who you are

from a group of poems thinking about Anne Sexton
on the anniversary of her death

> *"Look, you con man, make a living
> out of your death."*
>
> *Hemingway*

Questions for Anne

Did your poems write you like nightmares:

Did they play "shuffle-off-to-Buffalo" like the
Ames Bros.:

Did they dry up like Whaleback Waddy:

One night, did you come home
to toast your toes in front of them
& did they leave you cold:

Did they leave you in the lurch
like a teen-aged poppa:

Anne,

We are your children,

Where is the note, explaining. . . .

Answers from Anne

yes.　my poems dreamed me like nightmares—

yes.　they ended me like a cheap novel—

yes.　they played music on my backbones. fish butchers.

　　　　i was their ankh, their xylophone
　　　　they owned me "Z" to "A"

　　　　THEY were the artist

　　　　i was the whore　the canvas

　　　　i was ivory keys—
　　　　their beast of 5 fingers

but when the time came, nothing could stop me, i tell you:

i made a living of my death

ms. claus

i am jolly   i am round as an apple
but larger   i
live in the attic beating
cookies into sugary little men
i cut them clean with their icings
spiffy jackets & button brown
raisin eyes
Santa gets a piece of ass once a week
i shop at Eskimo
A & P

unburying the bird

buried birds
are usually
dead.
fallen from the sky
because of too much
something.
    too much high.
    too much steep.
    too much long.
    too much deep.
but sometimes
one has been known
to go underground.
you do not hear a peep
for years.
then one day,
you go back to the spot
thinking you will not find
a feather or a few
scattered bones
& you hear something
pecking   trying
to get out of there.
you are afraid to believe
it is still alive.
afraid that even if it is
in being freed, it will die.
still,
slowly,
you go about freeing the bird.

you scrape away the grave
which in some mysterious way
has not suffocated her.
you free her scrawny head.
her dangling wing.
you keep thinking her body
must be broken beyond healing.
you keep thinking the delicate
instruments of flight
will never pull again.
still,
you free her.
feed her from the tip of your finger.
teach her the cup of your hand.
you breathe on her.
one day,
you open up your hand
& show her sky.

ABOUT THE AUTHOR

Toi Derricotte was born in Detroit on April 12, 1941 and grew up in a black, middle-class section of the city. Her mother, who had come to Detroit from Louisiana, is of Creole stock, and her paternal grandmother was a tall, red-haired woman who was proud of her "German blood." Her grandfather, the owner of Webster's Funeral Home, belonged to a prestigious family of "old Detroiters."

Of her early associations, the author writes: "I sensed a paranoia in the adults in my childhood, a pervasive sense of vulnerability, of living in a threatening, unpredictable, inconsistent, and personally hostile universe. Perhaps these were only my own feelings which I projected onto these adults, but it may also have something to do with the fact that being black in a 'white' world is like having a reasonless and frightening parent—a huge man who might snap out and kill you for nothing or for something you can't do anything about. Most of the people who lived in the neighborhood I grew up in had just escaped the ghettoes of the city and the sense of the absolute vulnerability of the poor was more than a memory, it was palpable. Their rigid and compulsive adherence to monetary goals was their only hope for survival and their only hope of giving their children some degree of independence from those threatening forces that had controlled their life."

Mrs. Derricotte married at the age of eighteen, bore a son the following year, and obtained a divorce at twenty-two, the same year she received her bachelor's degree at Wayne State University. After teaching for five years, she remarried and moved to New York City, where her continuing education included several years' participation in writers' workshops. While she was a graduate student at New York University, she was awarded first prize in the Academy of American Poets competition. Other recognition followed.

Presently a resident of Montclair, New Jersey, the poet has been active as teacher and editor and has presented numerous readings. For the past four years she has been involved in the Poets-in-the-Schools program sponsored by the New Jersey State Council on Art. Her poems have appeared in a number of magazines and anthologies. *The Empress of the Death House* is the first collection of her work.